THE *Choir* AND THE *Organ* IN EARLY LUTHERANISM

DANIEL ZAGER
STEVEN WENTE

Lutheran University Press
Minneapolis, Minnesota

The Choir and the Organ in Early Lutheranism
Daniel Zager & Steven Wente

Published under the auspices of the:
Center for Church Music
Concordia University Chicago
River Forest, IL 60305-1402

ISBN: 978-1-942304-28-9

Lutheran University Press
PO Box 390759
Minneapolis, MN 55439
Manufactured in the United States of America

Contents

About the Center for Church Music

The Center for Church Music was established in 2010 on the campus of Concordia University Chicago. Its purpose is to provide ongoing research and educational resources in Lutheran church music, especially in the areas of congregational song and composition for the Church. It is intended to be of interest to pastors, musicians, and laity alike.

The Center maintains a continually expanding resource room that houses the Schalk American Lutheran Hymnal Collection, the manuscript collections of prominent Lutheran composers and hymn writers, and a broad array of reference works and resources in church music. To create a global awareness and facilitate online research, efforts are underway to digitize the hymnal collection, the manuscript archives, and the hymn festival recordings.

The Center publishes monographs and books covering various aspects of Lutheran church music.

The Center maintains a dynamic website whose features include devotions, presentations, oral histories, biographical essays, resource recommendations, and conversations on various topics in worship and church music.

The Center's Founders Group includes Linda and Robert Kempke, Nancy and Bill Raabe, Mary and Charles Sukup, and Waldemar B. Seefeldt, whose significant monetary gifts initiated the Center and have, along with the gifts of many others, sustained its momentum.

The Center's Advisory Board includes James Freese, Scott Hyslop, Linda Kempke, Jonathan Kohrs, Nancy Raabe, Carl Schalk, Steven Wente, and Paul Westermeyer.

Barry L. Bobb serves as the Center's volunteer director.

You can follow news about the Center on Facebook. Learn more about the Center and subscribe to its free e-newsletter at https://cuchicago.edu/about-concordia/center-for-church-music

Preface

The celebration of the 500th anniversary of the Reformation brings with it an increased interest in all things Lutheran. Certainly one area of well-deserved attention is the rich tradition of a vibrant musical life in Lutheran congregations. This heritage—which continues to be lovingly passed from generation to generation—is due, in part, to the value Dr. Luther himself placed on music in worship.

Because the organ and the choir continue to play a significant role in the ministry of most Lutheran churches today, it would be easy to assume that this has always been the case. Not necessarily so.

The Center for Church Music wishes to thank both these scholars for expanding on presentations they made at the annual Lectures in Church Music at Concordia University Chicago in October of 2016. Both essays, in a lucid and thorough manner, paint the picture of the role of the organ and the choir in early Lutheran worship, thus dispelling a number of myths and assumptions that things "have always been this way" and offering some useful reflections on what this all means for the faithful practice of church music in our own time.

Barry L. Bobb

The Choir and Its Music in the Early Lutheran Reformation

As twenty-first-century Lutherans think back five centuries to the formative decades of the Lutheran church, there can be largely subconscious assumptions concerning what church life in the German-speaking lands of Europe might have been like as Martin Luther's ideas and writings were disseminated and printed. Such subconscious assumptions—in which we project our times, ideas, procedures, and customs backward to the early decades of the Lutheran Reformation—are perhaps understandable, even as they may be misleading, unhelpful, and ultimately untenable historically. Among other areas of German Reformation history, liturgy and church music are susceptible to such false assumptions. We might imagine, for example, that our sixteenth-century Lutheran forebears in Wittenberg held printed hymnals and sang the new vernacular hymns to the accompaniment of organs. And yet in Luther's time churches did not provide hymnals for congregants, organs were not used to accompany congregational singing, and indeed congregants only gradually learned to sing in church.[1] Or we might assume the inevitable and ubiquitous presence of choirs in the churches of the early Lutheran Reformation, for choirs within the Chris-

1 Such issues are treated in these studies: Robin A. Leaver, *"The Whole Church Sings": Congregational Singing in Luther's Wittenberg, 1523–1529* (Grand Rapids, Mich.: Eerdmans, 2017), *Organ Accompaniment of Congregational Song: Historical Documents and Settings, Part 1: Sixteenth and Seventeenth Centuries*, ed. Robin A. Leaver and Daniel Zager (Colfax, N.C.: Wayne Leupold Editions, 2017), Robin A. Leaver, *Luther's Liturgical Music: Principles and Implications* (Grand Rapids, Mich.: Eerdmans, 2007), Joseph Herl, *Worship Wars in Early Lutheranism: Choir, Congregation, and Three Centuries of Conflict* (New York: Oxford University Press, 2004).

tian liturgical tradition existed from early medieval times.[2] But that assumption, too, needs to be examined in historically nuanced ways that carefully distinguish among the following variables: 1) where choirs might have been found in early sixteenth-century German ecclesiastical establishments—whether in court chapels, parish churches (in cities or villages), or monastic establishments; 2) in what languages these choirs sang—Latin, German, or both; and 3) whether they sang polyphony, monophonic chant, or both. This essay, examining the choir in the early Lutheran Reformation, takes as its point of departure the music that choirs sang: both Latin-texted and German-texted, monophonic and polyphonic.

I begin by looking at what choirs, particularly in court chapels, sang just prior to the events of the Lutheran Reformation—examining what that movement *inherited* from the rich musical traditions of the Western church. Second, I consider Luther's attitudes toward the music of these inherited traditions, relying particularly on his liturgical writings from the 1520s. Third, I note his commitment to providing German-language psalms and hymns, and how that affected music for choirs. Among the Continental reformers Luther alone was receptive to various types of sacred music: chant *and* polyphony—both Latin- *and* German-texted, music for choirs *and* for congregations. I will illustrate the persistent influence of this inclusive attitude toward sacred music in the young Lutheran church by ranging further into the sixteenth century: noting the 1545 chant anthology compiled by Johann Spangenberg for the liturgical year, the music publications of the Wittenberg printer Georg Rhau, and finally a nod to the early seventeenth-century Lutheran cantor Michael Praetorius and his vast compositional output of both Latin- and German-texted music for the church. My goal is to offer an historical perspective that stresses: 1) early Lu-

2 The Roman schola cantorum was organized during the late seventh century, cf., among other secondary sources, James McKinnon, *The Advent Project: The Later Seventh-Century Creation of the Roman Mass Proper* (Berkeley: University of California Press, 2000), 86–89, 359–60.

theran *continuity* with the received musical traditions of the Western church, and 2) the simultaneous development of an essentially new genre—the vernacular hymn, the German chorale—which grew quickly and exponentially from its beginnings with Luther in 1523–1524.

Because music sung by choirs was not a new or innovative practice in the early Lutheran Reformation, it is important to begin consideration of this topic in the late fifteenth century and the first decades of the sixteenth century. Where would one find choirs during this time period? Powerful, wealthy rulers, like Maximilian I (1459–1519, Holy Roman Emperor 1493–1519), or Frederick the Wise (1463–1525, Elector of Saxony 1486–1525), maintained their own fully-staffed court chapels (Hofkapellen), including accomplished, professional singers and instrumentalists. Second, in cities and towns with Latin schools the boys were trained to sing the music of the Mass and Offices and did so in the local churches.[3] Third, in some monastic communities monks or nuns would have sung the music of Mass and Office liturgies.

What musical repertories would have been sung by these choirs? Here it is important to make a distinction between singing of monophonic and polyphonic music. The former—singing of unison chant—was known as singing *choraliter*. The latter—singing of polyphony—was known as singing *figuraliter*. The term *choraliter* refers to singing unmeasured chant (the German word *Choral* referring to chant), while the term *figuraliter* refers to measured music using various rhythmic values and in two or more parts. All choirs—whether attached to a court chapel, a city or town church, or a monastic establishment—would have sung *choraliter*. The choir of a court chapel would also have sung *figuraliter*, a type of music-making found in some parish churches as well during the sixteenth century.

3 That was the case, for example, at Wittenberg's Stadtkirche. See Leaver, *"The Whole Church Sings,"* chapter 7, and Marie Schlüter, *Musikgeschichte Wittenbergs im 16. Jahrhundert: Quellenkundliche und sozialgeschichtliche Untersuchungen*, Abhandlungen zur Musikgeschichte, Bd. 18 (Göttingen: V + Runipress, 2010), 49–64.

Perhaps because the writing of Western music history has tended to favor complex music, situated in a kind of "progress" paradigm, the history of Western *chant* in the German-speaking territories during the fifteenth and sixteenth centuries has not been studied nearly as thoroughly as the polyphonic music of that same period. Thus, we are able to be more precise about the music sung *figuraliter* compared to that sung *choraliter*—ironically perhaps, since the latter would have predominated quantitatively in terms of daily usage in the various ecclesiastical establishments during the decades leading up to the events of the Lutheran Reformation. Local chant sources of the fifteenth and sixteenth centuries (whether manuscript or printed) used in the German-speaking lands too often were not preserved, as liturgical needs changed and evolved during the sixteenth and seventeenth centuries. Precisely because liturgical practice was not standardized (in the Roman Catholic realm, for instance, not until after the Council of Trent, 1545–1563), *local* sources (by diocese and city) are so important, whether *textual* sources such as missals and breviaries (preserving *texts* for the Mass and Offices, respectively) or their *musical* counterparts—graduals and antiphonals (preserving *chants* for the Mass and Offices).

In her seminal study of liturgy and music at Wittenberg's Castle Church during the time of Frederick the Wise, Kathryn Ann Pohlmann Duffy notes "the absence of [local] missals and graduals from the Castle Church."[4] Subsequently, she examined liturgical books from the dioceses of Magdeburg, Brandenburg, Mainz, Meissen, and Passau, concluding that:

> . . . the liturgy of the Castle Church . . . was drawn from a variety of liturgical usages and did not adhere to the liturgy of any single usage. The repertory is clearly a German one. . . . Beyond this, however, it is difficult to ascertain which German

4 Kathryn Ann Pohlmann Duffy, "The Jena Choirbooks: Music and Liturgy at the Castle Church in Wittenberg under Frederick the Wise, Elector of Saxony" (Ph.D. diss., University of Chicago, 1995), 342.

> sources were most heavily relied upon for the formation of the liturgy in the Castle Church.[5]

We know that the choir in Wittenberg's Castle Church would have sung *choraliter*, that they sang the Latin chant of the Western church according to the annual round of the church year and the daily round of Mass and Office liturgies. But we do not possess sources preserving chant repertories specific to the Castle Church, sources equivalent to, for example, surviving books that preserve the chant repertories for Mass and Office liturgies from the Diocese of Passau: a 1511 printed gradual (preserving chants for the Mass) and a 1519 printed antiphonal (preserving chants for the Offices). Both sources were printed in Vienna, home to Emperor Maximilian's Hofkapelle. These sources are noteworthy for several reasons: 1) they preserve chant repertories exemplifying the music that a choir would have sung *choraliter* during the earliest years of the Lutheran Reformation (though, of course, these are not Wittenberg sources); 2) Elector Frederick the Wise would have heard Maximilian's Hofkapelle sing these repertories *choraliter* as he attended various Imperial Diets over the years; thus, 3) it is for good reason that Duffy cites the Diocese of Passau as one influence on the liturgies of Wittenberg's Castle Church; and 4) these Passau sources are readily available for browsing in digital form on the Internet—making it easy to see what such chant books look like.[6]

Thus, we know that choirs in pre-Reformation German-speaking territories sang Latin chant, and indeed did so in Frederick's Castle Church in Wittenberg, even if we cannot reconstruct that specific local chant repertory. But a crucial question is whether such pre-Reformation chant repertories

5 Ibid., 581.

6 Both of these chant sources are available as part of the VD 16 program (Verzeichnis der im deutschen Sprachbereich erschienennen Drucke des 16. Jahrhunderts): http://www.gateway-bayern.de/index_vd16/. The 1511 gradual is available digitally in VD 16 as item number G 2728, the 1519 antiphonal as item number A 2946. Both sources are also available as facsimiles in the printed series *Das erbe deutscher Musik*, Bd. 87 providing the gradual, and Bd. 88 the antiphonal.

continued to be sung by choirs in the earliest decades of the Lutheran Reformation, and indeed beyond those formative years. Here, Luther's attitudes toward the inherited traditions of Latin liturgy and chant are of critical importance.

* * *

In his 1523 *Von ordenung gottis diensts ynn der gemeyne* [Concerning the Order of Public Worship] Luther is very clear about Latin chant: "Let the chants in the Sunday masses and Vespers be retained; they are quite good and are taken from Scripture."[7] In December 1523 Luther published his more detailed *Formula missae* [An Order of Mass and Communion for the Church at Wittenberg], with additional commentary on chants for the Mass. He declares as "unobjectionable" the Introits, the Kyrie, the Gloria in Excelsis, the Graduals and Alleluias, the Sanctus, the Agnus Dei, and the proper Communion chants.[8] He does not approve Offertory chants, because they contributed to the false concept of the Lord's Supper as a sacrifice rather than a sacrament.[9] Indeed, he refers to the canon of the Mass as "that abominable concoction drawn from everyone's sewer and cesspool"[10] and the offertory as "that utter abomination."[11] He also allowed no sequences (with the exception of "Grates nunc omnes" at Christmas, and two sequence texts related to the Holy Spirit: "Sancti spiritus" and "Veni sancte spiritus").[12] Thus, with the exception of Offertory chants and the vast repertory of medieval sequences, Luther approved and welcomed Latin chant in the order of the Mass as he wished it to be observed in Wittenberg. Unlike the Swiss reformers, Luther welcomed continuity with the historic liturgy of the church—except where its texts caused theological error.

7 Martin Luther, *Liturgy and Hymns*, ed. Ulrich S. Leupold, Luther's Works: American Edition, vol. 53 (Philadelphia: Fortress Press, 1965), 13. This source is cited subsequently as LW 53.

8 Ibid., 21.

9 Ibid., 21–22.

10 Ibid., 21.

11 Ibid., 25–26.

12 Ibid., 25.

Three years later, in 1526, as Luther published his *Deutsche Messe und ordnung Gottis diensts* [The German Mass and Order of Service], he commented further on his desire to retain Latin liturgy and chant, referring to his *Formula missae* of three years earlier:

> It is not now my intention to abrogate or to change [the Latin] service. . . . For in no wise would I want to discontinue the service in the Latin language, because the young are my chief concern. And if I could bring it to pass, and Greek and Hebrew were as familiar to us as the Latin and had as many fine melodies and songs, we would hold mass, sing, and read on successive Sundays in all four languages, German, Latin, Greek, and Hebrew. I do not at all agree with those who cling to one language and despise all others. . . . It is also reasonable that the young should be trained in many languages; for who knows how God may use them in time to come? For this purpose our schools were founded.[13]

That choirs of the early Lutheran Reformation would continue to sing *choraliter* is due 1) to Luther's love for and approval of Latin chant repertories, and 2) to his pedagogical emphasis on the young learning the Latin language and subsequently applying that knowledge to singing this great musical treasure of the church.

One might contend that in the liturgical writings quoted above Luther is focusing on the *texts* of Latin chants rather than on the music. His love specifically for the *music* of the Latin chant tradition may be seen in his 1530 letter to the composer Ludwig Senfl (ca. 1489-91–1543).[14] In this letter Luther makes a specific request of Senfl, writing that he has always found delight in the chant antiphon "In pace in idipsum, dormiam et requiescam," Psalm 4:8 ("In peace I will

13 Ibid., 62–63.

14 Martin Luther, *Letters II*, ed. and trans. Gottfried G. Krodel, Luther's Works: American Edition, vol. 49 (Philadelphia: Fortress Press, 192), 427–29.

both lie down and sleep").[15] Luther asks Senfl for a polyphonic setting of this text:

> I ask if you would have copied and sent to me, if you have it, a copy of that song: "In peace [I will both lie down and sleep]." For this tenor melody has delighted me from youth on, and does so even more now that I understand the words.

The phrase "tenor melody" refers to the preexistent Latin chant, which, in a newly composed polyphonic setting, was most often placed in the tenor part of the polyphonic complex, the part that quite literally "held" ("tenere") the chant melody. Luther continues:

> I have never seen this antiphon arranged for more voices [i.e., a polyphonic setting]. I do not wish, however, to impose on you the work of arranging; rather I assume that you have available an arrangement from some other source.[16]

Luther's first biographer, Johannes Mathesius (1504–1565), provides additional insight on this episode, reporting in his 1566 biography of Luther that Senfl did, in fact, provide a polyphonic setting of "In pace in idipsum," and, in addition, a polyphonic setting of Psalm 118:17, "Non moriar, sed vivam." Luther reciprocated by sending books to Senfl.[17] A four-part setting of "In pace in idipsum" is preserved anonymously in a set of manuscript partbooks from the mid-sixteenth century: Zwickau, Ratsschulbibliothek, Mus. Ms. 73. While this source includes thirteen polyphonic settings attributed by the copyist to Senfl, the setting of "In pace in idipsum" is not so designated. Thus, the setting may not be Senfl's, but it is important to remember that Luther did not wish to impose on Senfl for a new work; Luther assumed, or perhaps hoped, that Senfl was in possession of a polyphonic setting of this text by another composer.

15 Ibid., 428.

16 Ibid., 428–29.

17 Leaver, *Luther's Liturgical Music*, 52 and 369, note 204.

The significant point in Luther's letter to Senfl is that Luther makes clear his love for a particular chant melody, which, of course, accords well with his general love for music. Thus, when Luther speaks approvingly of chant in his liturgical writings from 1523 and 1526, we may understand those references as referring to both text and music of Latin chant—the large and strikingly beautiful musical repertory of the Western church that continued to constitute an important part of the repertory for choirs in the early Lutheran Reformation.

* * *

Luther also made clear in various writings his love for Latin *polyphonic* music, the music sung *figuraliter* by choirs. Of course, one piece of evidence is Luther's 1530 request to Senfl for a polyphonic setting of "In pace in idipsum." But apart from this request there are other bits of evidence for Luther's love of polyphonic music. On more than one occasion Luther pointed to Josquin des Prez (ca. 1450-55–1521), the preeminent composer of the later fifteenth and early sixteenth centuries, as a master of polyphonic composition. Recorded sometime before December 14, 1531 in the so-called "Table Talk," Luther stated that "God has preached the gospel through music, too, as may be seen in Josquin, all of whose compositions flow freely, gently, and cheerfully, and are not forced or cramped by rules like the song of the finch."[18] Also recorded in the "Table Talk," around 1540, is Luther's observation that "Josquin is a master of the notes, which must express what he desires; on the other hand, other . . . composers must do what the notes dictate."[19] Finally, one of Luther's most eloquent statements on polyphony may

18 Martin Luther, *Table Talk*, ed. Theodore G. Tappert, Luther's Works: American Edition, vol. 54 (Philadelphia: Fortress Press, 1967), 129–30. For a necessary corrective to Tappert's translation see Leaver, *Luther's Liturgical Music*, 368, note 199.

19 Walter E. Buszin, *Luther on Music*, Lutheran Society for Worship, Music and the Arts, Pamphlet Series, no. 3 (St. Paul, Minn.: North Central Publishing, 1958), 13 [reprinted from *Musical Quarterly* 32 (January, 1946].

be found in his preface to Georg Rhau's *Symphoniae iucundae* of 1538, itself an anthology of Latin polyphony:

> . . . it is possible to taste with wonder (yet not to comprehend) God's absolute and perfect wisdom in his wondrous works of music. Here it is most remarkable that one single voice continues to sing the tenor [i.e., the preexistent chant melody], while at the same time many other voices play around it, exulting and adorning it in exuberant strains. . . .[20]

In his great love for Latin polyphony Luther essentially set a precedent for the music sung by Lutheran choirs—not only of his time but for a lengthy and rich future touching our time as well. Luther made clear that the art music of the best composers of his time was, in fact, the music that he valued for the church's proclamation of the Gospel. He was not saying that only the most complex music of his time was what was required by the church. Instead, he assumed that well-crafted music by well-trained composers was to be the norm for the church's proclamation of the Gospel. But how did Luther know the music of Josquin? Where might he have become acquainted with the best of Latin sacred polyphony? Here we return to the pre-Reformation part of this inquiry.

That Luther was familiar with the magnificent and extensive Franco-Flemish repertory of fifteenth-century Latin sacred polyphony is due to Frederick the Wise, Elector of Saxony. Frederick established his chapel of clergy and musicians—the Hofkapelle—in 1491, their responsibility being to furnish music for the daily Mass and Office liturgies wherever Frederick was "in residence," whether traveling, or in Wittenberg or Torgau, the latter being his primary place of residence.

20 LW 53, 324.

In Wittenberg, Frederick's new Castle Church was dedicated on January 17, 1503, one year after he had established his new university in Wittenberg. Also known as the Allerheiligenstiftskirche, after the small Allerheiligenkapelle, or All Saints chapel, which previously occupied that site, the Castle Church had its own group of clergy and musicians responsible for an extensive daily round of Mass and Office liturgies, by Duffy's estimate "over 1,000 [sung] Masses each year."[21] That pattern remained until late 1524 when, at Luther's urging, "all the masses except for the evangelical Sunday mass were discontinued."[22]

Latin polyphony for those liturgical observances was provided by two groups of music manuscripts, those groups being distinguished one from the other by where they were copied. A total of nineteen manuscript sources of Latin polyphony used at the Castle Church have come down to us, all of which, save one, are now held by the university library in Jena (the one exception residing in Weimar). The first group of eight manuscripts[23] was copied between approximately 1500 and 1520 at the Castle Church in Wittenberg for use at that establishment.[24] These Wittenberg manuscripts preserve polyphony for both the Proper and Ordinary of the Mass as well as music for Vespers. The second group, consisting of eleven manuscripts,[25] was copied between 1500 and 1525 in the famed scriptoria of Petrus Alamire (ca. 1470–1536) and his associates (in present-day Belgium), and either presented to Frederick as gifts by Margaret of Austria or by her father Holy Roman Emperor Maximilian I, or purchased by

21 Duffy, 174.

22 Martin Brecht, *Martin Luther: Shaping and Defining the Reformation, 1521–1532*, trans. James L. Schaaf (Minneapolis: Fortress Press, 1994), 129. See Leaver, *"The Whole Church Sings,"* chapter 7, for consideration of the musical ramifications of this action.

23 Jena 30, 31, 32, 33, 34, 35, 36, and Weimar A.

24 Duffy, 2.

25 Jena 2, 3, 4, 5, 7, 8, 9, 12, 20, 21, and 22.

Frederick.[26] The Alamire manuscripts furnish predominantly music for the Ordinary of the Mass as well as settings of the Magnificat. Ten of the eleven Alamire manuscripts were copied on parchment rather than paper, and exquisite miniature decorative artwork characterizes these sources, as is typical of manuscripts from that workshop. In contrast to these Alamire manuscripts, the eight manuscripts produced in Wittenberg were copied on paper rather than parchment and show very little in the way of artistic miniature illuminations. All nineteen of the manuscripts are in so-called "choirbook" format, meaning that the singers gathered around a single choirbook, each singer focusing on his own voice part, for example: soprano and tenor parts are placed on the left-hand (verso) page of an opening, with alto and bass parts on the right-hand (recto) page of that same opening. It was up to the scribe to coordinate his copying of the separate voice parts so that at each page turn of the choirbook the voice parts coordinated perfectly with each other. These manuscript sources are emblematic of the music that Frederick provided for his Wittenberg chapel, the first two decades of the century being a time of intensive effort to acquire Latin polyphony in manuscript choirbooks for use at Wittenberg's Castle Church.

Of these nineteen manuscripts used at the Castle Church, five include works attributed to Josquin, primarily settings of the Mass Ordinary. Of the Alamire manuscripts Jena 3 includes five Mass Ordinaries securely attributed to Josquin, with one more in Jena 7 and two in Jena 21. Of the manuscripts copied in Wittenberg, Jena 31 and 32 each preserve

26 For a detailed study of this group of eleven manuscripts see Hannah Hutchens Mowrey, "The Alamire Manuscripts of Frederick the Wise: Intersections of Music, Art, and Theology" (PhD diss., Eastman School of Music, University of Rochester, 2010). For descriptions of each manuscript see *The Treasury of Petrus Alamire: Music and Art in Flemish Court Manuscripts, 1500–1535*, ed. Herbert Kellman (Ghent, Amsterdam: Ludion, 1999); the range of dates for these sources, 1500–1525, reflects the descriptions in this volume. Mowrey argues persuasively that the Alamire manuscripts were used at Frederick's Castle Church in Wittenberg rather than at his Hofkapelle; see pp. 362–77 of her dissertation.

three Mass Ordinaries by Josquin. From these manuscript sources alone it is clear that Luther had ample opportunity to hear the music of Josquin; indeed, in the Mass Ordinaries preserved in these sources one finds some of Josquin's finest polyphony for the church. This pre-reformation Wittenberg polyphonic repertory provided an important precedent for choirs in the early Lutheran Reformation. Given Luther's love for polyphonic music, and specifically for the music of Josquin that he would have heard at the Castle Church, there could be no doubt that polyphonic music would become an important part of the repertory for early Lutheran choirs.

* * *

Near the end of his 1523 *Formula missae*, after describing and commenting on the Latin Mass as he wished it to be observed in Wittenberg, Luther also called for German-language hymns:

> I also wish that we had as many songs as possible in the vernacular which the people could sing during mass, immediately after the gradual and also after the Sanctus and Agnus Dei. For who doubts that originally all the people sang these which now only the choir sings or responds to while the bishop [pastor] is consecrating? The bishops [pastors] may have these [congregational] hymns sung either after the Latin chants, or use the Latin on one [Sun]day and the vernacular on the next, until the time comes that the whole mass is sung in the vernacular. But poets are wanting among us, or not yet known, who could compose evangelical and spiritual songs, as Paul calls them [Col. 3:16], worthy to be used in the church of God.[27]

While this essay is not the appropriate place to review the early development of the German chorale, suffice it to say

27 LW 53, 36.

that this call dating from December 1523 was answered in 1524 by the publication of the earliest collections of chorales: 1) a collection of eight hymns (four by Luther) printed in Nuremberg (the so-called "Achtliederbuch"), and 2) two Erfurt hymnals, both containing the same twenty-six hymn texts and both entitled "Enchiridion." These volumes contained music notation for some (though not all) of the chorale melodies.[28]

Another 1524 publication provided *polyphonic* settings of this newly emerging repertory of German chorales: Johann Walter's (1496–1570) *Geystliche gesangk Buchleyn*.[29] It is absolutely remarkable that polyphonic settings for choir appeared so early in the history of the chorale; certainly, it is testimony to Walter's ability as a composer. On the other hand, one could argue that—apart from Walter's fluent grasp of the polyphonic musical language of his time—there is nothing remarkable at all about this publication, since it followed in a well-established tradition of polyphony for choirs. Walter's accomplishment was not only in producing this collection so quickly but in doing so with German instead of Latin texts. While we might assume that Walter could write polyphonic settings of German texts as readily as Latin texts, we should not simply take that for granted. Similarly, in sixteenth-century England we take for granted that the composer Thomas Tallis (ca. 1505–1585), after writing Latin polyphony for the church, was able suddenly to switch gears and compose English anthems—a new genre—for the ver-

28 A facsimile of the 1524 *Etlich Cristlich Lider* ("Achtliederbuch") was distributed as a supplement to *Jahrbuch für Liturgik und Hymnologie* 2 (1956) (Kassel: Johannes Stauda-Verlag, 1957) and 50 (2011) (Göttingen: Vandenhoeck & Ruprecht, 2011). For the Erfurt publications, see *Das Erfurter Enchiridion*, Documenta Musicologica, Erste Reihe: Druckschriften-Faksimiles, no. 36 (Kassel: Bärenreiter, 1983).

29 A facsimile edition of the 1525 printing is available (no exemplar of the 1524 printing has survived): Johann Walter, *Das geistliche Gesangbüchlein: "Chorgesangbuch,"* Faksimile-Nachdruck des Zweitdruckes Worms 1525, ed. Walter Blankenburg, Documenta musicologica, 1. Reihe, Druckschriften-Faksimiles, 33 (Kassel: Bärenreiter, 1979).

nacular liturgy during the reign of Edward VI (1547–1553). In both cases, composers who were masters of their craft accomplished the transition from Latin to the vernacular. Of course, the significant difference in Germany is Luther's desire to retain Latin-texted music (both *choraliter* and *figuraliter*) while adding to the mix German-language chorales and their polyphonic elaborations. The conceptual triumph—welcoming the full panoply of Latin-texted and German-texted music in the liturgy—is Luther's; the compositional triumph of furnishing polyphonic settings of the new German chorales already in 1524—is Walter's.

Walter's experience at Frederick's electoral chapel in Torgau brought him into contact with Franco-Flemish polyphony of the late fifteenth and early sixteenth centuries. That experience and training enabled him to write German polyphonic settings modeled on and rooted in the Latin polyphonic tradition. Lutheran choirs in Torgau, Wittenberg, and elsewhere during the sixteenth century thus became heirs of a newly enriched tradition that combined Latin chant and polyphony with the German chorale and its associated polyphonic repertories.

Walter's 1524 collection, published in five partbooks, contained forty-three settings for three, four, and five voices, typically with the preexistent melody in the tenor part. Of these forty-three settings, thirty eight were settings of German chorales and five were of Latin texts. Subsequent editions of this collection appeared in 1525, 1528, 1534, 1537, 1544, and 1551. In his study of music in early Lutheranism, Carl Schalk points out that "by the last edition of 1551 the number of Latin pieces had grown to forty-seven," thus underscoring the continuing importance of Latin polyphony for early Lutheran choirs, even in the face of the developing repertories of German chorales and their subsequent polyphonic elaborations.[30]

30 Carl Schalk, *Music in Early Lutheranism: Shaping the Tradition (1524–1672)* (St. Louis: Concordia Academic Press, 2001), 31.

* * *

How does Luther's expansive view of music fare past these early years of the Lutheran Reformation, particularly with regard to music for choirs? I will consider that question by referring to: 1) Johann Spangenberg's chant anthology from 1545, 2) the Wittenberg printer Georg Rhau's publications for choir printed between 1538 and 1545, and 3) the vast published output of Michael Praetorius printed between 1605 and 1621.

During the course of the sixteenth century Lutheran choirs continued to sing *choraliter*, that is, they continued to sing unison chant. One year before Luther's death in 1546 Johann Spangenberg (1484–1550) published a substantial anthology of chants for the entire church year. This anthology was actually two volumes in one, with separate title pages for each part of the collection. The first part was entitled *Cantiones ecclesiasticae* and contained Latin chants for the church year. The second part was entitled *Kirchengesenge Deudsch* and contained German-language chants and chorales for the church year.[31] *Cantiones ecclesiasticae* would have been useful in cities and towns with Latin schools, where the choir of boys would have been trained to sing these chants in church. *Kirchengesenge Deudsch* would have been useful in towns and villages without Latin schools, where only German was spoken. Spangenberg's volume is a large one and could have been placed on a stand so that the Kantor and choirboys could gather around and see the music notation—similar to, for example, the Castle Church choirbooks of Latin polyphony.

31 For background on Spangenberg's chant anthology see: Daniel Zager, "Music for the Lutheran Liturgy: Johann Spangenberg's *Cantiones ecclesiasticae/Kirchengesenge Deudtsch* (1545), in *This Is the Feast: A Festschrift for Richard Hillert at 80*, ed. James Freese (St. Louis: MorningStar Music Publishers, 2004), 45–60; Robin A. Leaver, "Johann Spangenberg and Luther's Legacy of Liturgical Chant," *Lutheran Quarterly* 19 (Spring 2005): 23–42; and Jonathan Wessler, "An Examination of the Relationship Between Johann Spangenberg's *Cantiones ecclesiasticae/Kirchengensenge deudsch* and Martin Luther's *Formula missae et communionis* and *Deutsche Messe* (DMA diss., Eastman School of Music, 2011) http://hdl.handle.net/1802/15947.

Cantiones ecclesiasticae begins with the First Sunday of Advent, where Spangenberg provides a rather full set of chants: Introit, Kyrie, and Gloria in excelsis are all notated. Both the Epistle and Gospel lessons are fully notated as illustrations of lesson tones, with the Alleluia coming between these lessons (no sequence is provided; recall that Luther in his *Formula missae* of 1523 effectively did away with the vast repertory of medieval sequences). The Creed follows the Gospel, taking fully three-and-one-half pages for its complete notation. For Advent 1 Spangenberg also provided Latin chant for the Preface, the Sanctus, and the Agnus Dei.

Within *Cantiones ecclesiasticae* Advent 1 receives a particularly fulsome provision of Latin chant. The Creed, for example, is provided uniquely there. Pages for the subsequent Sundays in Advent provide only the texts of the Epistle and Gospel lessons; the Kantor would simply refer back to Advent 1 for the notated chants for the Advent season. Similar to Advent 1, Spangenberg used the festivals of Christmas and Easter as occasions for more comprehensive selections of notated Latin chant. He provided a complete set of chants for the Communion service only at Advent 1, Christmas, and Easter—the same occasions for which he provided new music each time for the Kyrie, Gloria, and Epistle and Gospel lesson tones.

Just as *Cantiones ecclesiasticae* follows Luther's *Formula missae*, so also Spangenberg's *Kirchengesenge Deudsch* follows the outline of Luther's *Deutsche Messe.* Again, Advent 1 begins this part of the volume and receives a quite fulsome provision of notated, monophonic German chant and chorales. In his *Deutsche Messe* Luther specified: "To begin the service we sing a hymn or a German Psalm in the First Tone";[32] Spangenberg provides the chorale "Komm Heiliger Geist, Herre Gott." The Kyrie is followed by Nikolaus Decius's chorale "Allein Gott in der Höh sei Ehr." The Epistle lesson is fully notated using very nearly the identical formula provided in Luther's *Deutsche Messe.* After the Epistle lesson Luther specified a German

32 LW 53, 69.

hymn, "either [Nun bitten wir] or any other, is sung with the whole choir."[33] For Advent 1 Spangenberg provides all stanzas of "Nun komm, der Heiden Heiland." The Gospel lesson, like the Epistle, is closely related to what Luther had provided in the *Deutsche Messe*. The Creed consists of the three stanzas of the chorale "Wir glauben all an einen Gott." In the communion liturgy that follows, the Preface is chanted, followed by the German Sanctus "Jesaia, dem Propheten." The chant for the Words of Institution is virtually identical to Luther's formula in the *Deutsche Messe*. Spangenberg specifies the same two chorales as Luther did for singing during the distribution of the Lord's Body and Blood: "Jesus Christus unser Heiland" and "Gott sei gelobet und gebenedeiet." Spangenberg also provides three additional chorales: the Agnus Dei is the chorale "O Lamm Gottes, unschuldig," following the Benediction the chorale "Verleih uns Frieden gnediglich," and after the concluding collect the chorale "Erhalt uns, Herr, bei deinem Wort." In *Kirchengesenge Deudsch* Advent 1 includes a complete collection of music for the Divine Service. Similar to the pattern in *Cantiones ecclesiasticae*, only the texts of the Epistle and Gospel lessons are then provided for the subsequent Sundays of Advent.

Thus, one year before Luther's death, we find an extensive printed anthology of music to be sung *choraliter*—both Latin and German, for the entire church year, and, notably, patterned after Luther's *Formula missae* and *Deutsche Messe*. Nor was Spangenberg's volume the only such collection providing Latin and German chant for Lutheran choirs. Throughout the second half of the sixteenth century further collections were produced for the Lutheran church:

> 1553 Nuremberg (subsequent editions: 1561, 1569, 1579, 1580, 1595)
> Lucas Lossius
> *Psalmodia, hoc est cantica sacra veteris ecclesiae selecta*

33 Ibid., 74.

1573 Wittenberg
Johannes Keuchenthal
Kirchen Gesenge Latinisch und Deudsch

1587 Leipzig
Nikolaus Selnecker
Christliche Psalmen, Lieder und Kirchengesenge

1588 Hamburg
Franz Eler
Cantica sacra

1589 Wittenberg
Matthäus Ludecus
Missale (2 vols.)
Vesperale et matutinale (1 vol.)
Psalterium Davidis (1 vol.)

At the death of Elector Frederick the Wise in 1525 his brother John the Steadfast succeeded him and disbanded both the Hofkapelle in Torgau and the musical establishment at the Castle Church, considering them too expensive to maintain. This action did not, however, signal the end of polyphonic music for choirs in early Lutheranism. The next decades would see an impressive effort to collect and publish polyphony for use in churches of the Lutheran confession.

Particularly important in this respect is the Wittenberg printer and musician Georg Rhau (1488–1548). As a musician Rhau wrote instructional music theory treatises covering both *musica choralis* (chant) and *musica figuralis* (polyphony). From 1518 to 1520 he served as cantor of Leipzig's St. Thomas school, the same position that J. S. Bach would hold a little over two centuries later. Rhau also lectured in music theory at the University of Leipzig. This pedagogical outlook on music, both as a teacher and as a music theorist, would serve him well as he returned to Wittenberg in 1523 to work as a printer and publisher. Since he had taught music to boys in a Latin school, and had written instructional materials on music theory, he was well positioned to provide repertories of vocal music for the young Lutheran church. He did so through fifteen collections published between 1538 and 1545.[34] It is important to understand that he not only participated in the printing process, but, of first importance, he actively selected the repertory contained in these sources, thus using his expertise as a Lutheran cantor and as a learned music theorist. J. Michael Raley writes that "Rhau's collections were designed to serve three principal purposes: (1) to provide the liturgical materials needed by local congregations who wished to observe the Lutheran mass and offices (principally vespers), (2) to supply musical and biblical training to boys in the city schools who also served in the choirs of their local churches, and (3) to foster the musical and spiritual edification of parishioners within their own homes."[35] In all, between 1538 and 1545 Rhau published fifteen collections of music: four for the Mass, six for Vespers, and five for other purposes. All of the volumes for the Mass and for Vespers contain Latin polyphony, as does the 1538 *Symphoniae iucundae*, a collection of fifty-two Latin motets. Two collections provide German polyphony. The 1544 *Newe deudsche geistliche Gesenge . . . für die gemeinen Schulen* includes 123 compositions, showing how the chorale was treated polyphonically twenty years after Walter's pathbreaking polyphonic settings of 1524. Rhau's collections of two-part and three-part settings, the *bicinia* and *tricinia* collections from 1542 and 1545, were intended to teach the boys to sing independently in two- and three-part textures—a first step toward developing the fluency in singing in four and more parts that they would need to sing polyphonic repertories for the Mass and Vespers.

---

34 For a summary of these publications—their liturgical content and representative composers included in each volume—see Schalk, 56–62. The collected edition is: *Musikdrucke aus den Jahren 1538 bis 1545 in praktischer Neuausgabe* (Kassel: Bärenreiter; St. Louis: Concordia Publishing House, 1955–1999).

35 J. Michael Raley, "Traversing Borders—Defining Boundaries: Cosmopolitan Harmonies and Confessional Theology in Georg Rhau's Liturgical Publications," *Sixteenth Century Journal* 43 (2012): 1081.

While Georg Rhau and Johann Walter both knew Luther and worked with him, Michael Praetorius (1571–1621) was a generation removed, his father having worked with Walter at the Latin school in Torgau. Were there to be the designation "greatest Lutheran cantor of all time," it would not necessarily be J. S. Bach; Michael Praetorius would surely be in the running. A prolific writer on music, and composer of both Latin- and German-texted music for the Lutheran church, Praetorius was systematic in assembling these repertories for Lutheran choirs.[36] Separate volumes from 1611 contain polyphonic settings for the Mass, settings of the Magnificat, and Latin hymns for Vespers, while a 1607 collection provides Latin motets. But perhaps his greatest achievement consists in the nine parts of *Musae Sioniae*, an encyclopedic collection of his own German chorale settings—over 1,200 compositions in total, ranging from straightforward cantional settings to elaborate polychoral settings.

* * *

As a music historian I find, not surprisingly, that historical study is its own reward. But that does not preclude asking what twenty-first-century Lutheran church musicians might learn from studying the first century of Lutheran music for choirs. And from that study what principles might we apply to our work with parish choirs?

First, we should note Luther's respect for, and embrace of, the musical traditions of the Western church. He was clearly interested in liturgical and musical *continuity* with the past. He had no interest in what Carl Schalk once memorably termed "a rootless now."

Second, he discerned the very best music of his time, for example, the music of Josquin and Senfl. Musical craftsmanship, compositional control, beauty mattered to Luther. He was unapologetic in expecting high levels of musical quality, and in claiming precisely that music for use in the proclamation of the Gospel.

36 See Schalk, 110–12, for a summary of Praetorius's works.

Third, I want to reflect briefly on Lutheran choirs singing *choraliter*, that is, the choir singing monophonically as well as polyphonically, unison as well as in parts. My observation—and I freely admit not based on a broad sampling of Lutheran parishes—is that our choirs today take few opportunities to sing in unaccompanied unison, or perhaps have little desire to do so. It is probably not totally off base to link that reality to another, namely, that our choirs too infrequently sing proper portions of the liturgy, occasions when they might, in fact, sing unison music. Early Lutheran choirs sang *choraliter* and *figuraliter*; we could, I suspect, do more with the former. While taking care not to paint with too broad a brush, I suspect that too many Lutheran parish choirs continue to focus more or less exclusively on singing an anthem during the offering. So as we ponder the music sung by choirs in the early Lutheran Reformation, we might think about whether and how we are using our choirs to sing (beautifully!) in unison, especially proper portions of the Divine Service: Introits, Psalms (with antiphons), Graduals, Verses, and *alternatim* hymn stanzas.

Finally, a study of music for choirs from the first century of the Lutheran church serves to remind us just how rich is our heritage as Lutheran church musicians—a musical heritage, moreover, that is constantly being added to and renewed by living composers. Thanks are due to Concordia University Chicago, and its Center for Church Music, for the role they have played and continue to play in reminding us of this heritage, and in encouraging its continuing use as Gospel proclamation in the twenty-first-century church.

The Organ in the Early Lutheran Reformation

The topic of the role of the organ in early Lutheran liturgies is one that may not be considered by many organists or others interested in church music. That it was possible for a worshiper in 1520s Wittenberg not to hear the organ is perhaps never considered. We may assume, however incorrectly, that the use of the organ at that time might not have been much different from the role of the organ at present.

I want to offer sincere thanks to Dr. Carl Schalk for the invitation to present this topic. I also would like to acknowledge the work of Dr. Herbert Gotsch, late professor of music at Concordia University Chicago, who explored the use of the organ and its literature in the early Lutheran church. This presentation began with a review of an article that Dr. Gotsch wrote for the journal *Church Music* (67.1).

To better understand the role of the organ, we will address several different questions:

1. How was the organ used before the Reformation?
2. What changed after the Reformation in how the organ was used?
3. What did Luther and others say about the organ?
4. What are some examples of early organ music for the liturgy?
5. How might the organ have come to "accompany" the singing of the hymns?

In this paper we will consider the use of the organ in the liturgy, not the full range of organ literature and possibilities. At the outset, there are a few general principles that should be considered:

> Some variety of practice certainly existed from location to location, given that each municipality had its own church order.
>
> New developments tended to happen in the cities and then spread to smaller towns.
>
> Developments in the use of the organ tended to follow vocal or choral practice.
>
> The orders describe what the practice should be; we have to assume that these rubrics were followed.

For the most part, this paper treats the use of the organ only in the German lands.

How was the organ used before the Reformation?

Our understanding of the organ as an instrument for use in the liturgy draws primarily from two sources: ecclesial documents which detail how the organ was to be used, and in some cases the presence of musical scores. It seems that at least in certain areas the role of the organ may have been fairly extensive.

In his dissertation *The Liturgical Use of the Organ in German Regions Prior to the Protestant Reformation: Contracts, Consuetudinaries, and Musical Repertories*, Douglas Earl Bush presents a number of documents about the use of the organ. For example, a "Rules for Playing the Organ" comes from the monastery of St. Bartholomew in Frankfort am Main, dating likely from the middle of the 14th century:

> Rules for Playing the Organ:
>
> Let this manner be observed in playing the organ and singing at the same time...At the Mass

> the organ and the choir will alternately perform only the *Kyrie eleison* and the sequence, with the organ beginning and likewise terminating... But an antiphon, or a part of it, which is played on the organ and which is immediately followed by a hymn played on the organ, should be repeated by the choir in order to make a pause between the antiphon and the hymn...[37]

Similarly in the daily office, directions for the organist were fairly specific. For example, at St. Martin's Church in Tiel, Gelderland (in the Netherlands region) in the early 16th c., there are specifications for playing at Vespers and Matins:

> First of all, the organist shall play at Mass and Vespers on Easter eve when the procession has come from the font. Also, likewise during the four holy days after Easter, he shall play the *Te Deum laudamus* at Matins, etc, also at Mass and at Vespers, and when they process to the font and as they bring the holy oil he shall play the *Te Deum laudamus*.

Following this is a listing of a number of feast days for which the *Te Deum* is played. [38]

Organ contracts of the time also specified the number of Sundays and feasts that the organist was to play. These contracts also might specify the expectations that the monastery or church might have of the organist, as an example from Memmingen, Bavaria (dated 1500) shows:

> Play on all Sundays and feast days as specified
>
> Be willing to play for weddings for whoever wants him to (with a specified honorarium)
>
> To supply the bellows workers for both organs at his own expense

37 Douglas Earl Bush, *The Liturgical Use of the Organ in German Regions Prior to the Protestant Reformation: Contracts, Consuetudinaries, and Musical Repertories*, (Ph. D. diss. University of Texas at Austin, 1982), 42.

38 Ibid., 71.

To take good care of the organs and keep them in tune[39]

Bush notes four different uses of the organ from a consuetudinary of 1336 from the cathedral church in Hamburg:[40]

1. Organ in alternation with the choir
2. organ as a solo instrument (here what is described is a specific piece, such as a responsory, or the *Felix namque*)
3. the organ as an accompaniment of the choir
4. the organ in alternation with soloists and the choir ("[the cantors] will sing one verse, and the choir sings a second, and the organ plays a third verse in alternation. At the end of Mass, all will sing together the *Ite, missa est...*"

On the matter of alternation, a typical pattern of performance for the nine-fold *Kyrie* and *Gloria* is found in the *Augsburger Orgelbuch* (1511):

Kyrie

1. Kyrie: organ	4. Christe: choir	7. Kyrie: organ
2. Kyrie: choir	5. Christe: organ	8. Kyrie: choir
3. Kyrie: organ	6. Christe: choir	9. Kyrie: organ

Gloria

1.	priest intones "*Gloria in excelsis Deo*")	
2.	*et in terra...*	organ
3.	*gratias agimus...*	choir
4.	*Domine Deus, Rex caelestis...*	organ
5.	*Domine Fili...*	choir
6.	*Domine Deus, Agnus Dei...*	organ
7.	*qui tollis...*	organ
8.	*qui sedes...*	choir
9.	*quoniam tu solus...*	choir
10.	*cum Sancto Spiritu...*	organ

39 Ibid., 57-58.

40 Ibid., 86.

The *Sanctus* and the *Agnus Dei* were similarly divided up for alternation.[41]

Other pre-Reformation sources for music include Arnolt Schlick's *Tabulaturen etlicher Lobgesang* (1512), the *Buxheimer Orgelbuch* (pieces written between 1460-1470), and the *Fundamentum* of Hans Buchner (also known as Hans von Constanz). Buchner's *Fundamentum* is of particular interest to organists because it is one of the earliest tutors (methods) on organ playing. In his volume Buchner gives numerous fingering examples.

It should be noted that the use of the organ in alternation may have varied from location to location (one would need to have an organ, obviously) and that it was not anything particularly new compared to choral practice. The various polyphonic settings of the ordinary from Machaut to Dufay to Josquin all assume a practice of alternation between the plainsong chant and a polyphonic setting similar to that described above. If we assume that the use of the organ derived from this practice, the organ then substitutes for the polyphonic vocal/choral setting. The obvious difference is the assumption of the text in the organ part rather than hearing it audibly.

What changed after the Reformation in how the organ was used?

There were no dramatic changes in the use of the organ, though various reformers expressed concern about the organ and placed specific limits on its use. Certainly, the advent of the Lutheran chorale did not immediately suggest the use of the organ to accompany. That was to come later. Herbert Gotsch notes that "nowhere does [Luther] recognize the organ as capable of making any contribution to the role of music in the service." He notes further that the church order prepared by Johannes Bugenhagen and Justas Jonas refers to the organ: "they are to use the organs (where such already

41 Ibid., 96-97.

exist), if they wish, only on Sunday for the *Te Deum laudamus* and whenever they sing German hymns." And further, "However, they ought not employ the organ in the Mass itself." [42] Yet, there are examples of a more expansive use of the organ. Gotsch gives an observation by Wolfgang Musculus, a pastor from Augsburg, visiting Wittenberg in 1536 (Exaudi Sunday, May 28), which describes the Introit, the *Kyrie eleison* and the *Gloria in excelsis* sung in alternation by verse with choir and organ, and the organ playing intonations for two hymns.[43]

Robert Marshall and Robin Leaver note that:

> Luther and other Protestant theologians were wary of its secular associations and disapproved of displays of virtuosity. Accordingly, they rejected autonomous organ music in the church service. Rather the entire liturgical repertory was available to the instrument; and Protestant organists, adopting a long-standing tradition, prepared intabulations of polyphonic vocal pieces..., typically adding idiomatic passages and embellishments to the original compositions.[44]

Gotsch provides an outline from the *Kirchenordnung* from Rostock in Mecklenburg, noting that the choice of the German verb *schlahen* indicates likely alternation.

> The *Kyrie* ought to be sung and played. The *Gloria in excelsis* ought to be intoned by a preacher, whereupon the organist should play, and the choir should sing: "All Glory Be to God on High" or *Et in terra pax hominibus*.

---

42 Herbert Gotsch, "The Organ in the Lutheran Service of the 16th Century," *Church Music* 67.1, quoting Emil Sehling, *Die evangelischen Kirchenordnungen des XVI. Jahrhunderts, vol. 1, 699,* 7.

43 Ibid., 7. The entire quote from Wolfgang Musculus visit is found in Robin Leaver and Daniel Zager, *Organ Accompaniment of Congregational Song: Historical Documents and Settings, Part 1*, (*Historical Organ Techniques and Repertoire*, vol. 12, Colfax, NC: Wayne Leupold Editions, 2017), 15.

44 Robert L. Marshall and Robin A. Leaver, "Chorale Settings," in *Oxford Music Online*, accessed October 20, 2016.

> After the epistle the sequence hymns or other psalms should on occasion be sung, and the organist should join in the music making.
>
> An intonation to the German Creed is indicated. The priest would sing:
>
> "I Believe in One God" in German or Latin, whereupon the organist should join in the music making; the people should sing the entire Creed, "We All Believe in One True God."
>
> ...the choir should sing the *Sanctus* in German or Latin or the hymn *Isaiah, Mighty Seer*, and the organist should join in the music making.
>
> Thereupon the organist should play and the congregation should sing *Jesus Christ, Our Blessed Savior*, and in addition, if there are many communicants, *O Lord, We Praise Thee* and *Help Me, O My God.*[45]

Thus, it seems that while the Lutheran Reformers were cautious about the use of the organ, the actual practice in many cases was more expansive and reflected a broader use of the organ in the liturgy. The primary function of the organ was to play an intonation to the singing or in alternation with the singing.

The repertory for the early Lutheran organist, then, consisted of 1) short versets played in alternation with the choir; 2) brief introductions to choral motets (with the express purpose of setting the pitch) and 3) intabulations, or keyboard arrangements of pre-existing motets. Soon the possibility of intabulation was applied to the new hymn melodies being composed, the Lutheran chorale.

45 Gotsch, 8.

What are some examples of early organ music for the liturgy?

Because organists were expected to be able to improvise, printed literature for the organ did not appear as readily as chorale settings for choirs. However, in the earliest generation of the Reformation, sources include collections by Hans Buchner who seems to have served only in Catholic provinces, and three others of Buchner's generation: Hans Kotter (c. 1485–1541), Leonhard Kleber (c. 1495–1556), and Fridolin Sicher (1490–1546), all of whom lived within the "Luther years." The repertory in these tablatures is largely based on vocal models, that is, intabulations of vocal works. Some pre-Reformation vernacular hymns, such as "In dulci jubilo" and "Resonet in laudibus" are included. The two earliest organ settings of Lutheran chorales appear to be "Komm, heiliger Geist" in Kleber's tablature[46] and "Aus tiefer Not" in Kotter's.[47] A few examples of intabulations may be found in collections of general service music readily available to the organist.[48]

Early collections of chorale settings for keyboard were called tablatures, because the keyboard notation used letters rather than notes on a staff. Tablatures in the German lands were either old German or new German. The old German tablatures, such as Buchner, Kotter and Kleber), used a staff with notes for the upper voice and letters for the lower voice. The "new" German tablature used letter notation solely as seen in Figure 1.

---

46 John Butt, "Germany and the Netherlands," in Alexander Silbiger, ed. *Keyboard Music Before 1700*, (New York: Schirmer books, An Imprint of Simon & Schuster Macmillan, 1995), 158.

47 Harlan McConnell, "The Sixteenth-Century German Keyboard Chorale," in *Church Music 75.1* (St. Louis, Mo: Concordia Publishing House, 1967), 14-15. McConnell provides a possible timeline of the two tablatures.

48 For example, in the *Concordia Hymn Prelude Series*, vols. 6 and 8 contain intabulations of Heinrich Isaac's "O Welt, ich muss dich lassen." The Faber Early Organ Series, especially volumes 11 and 13, contains examples of early intabulations and chorale preludes.

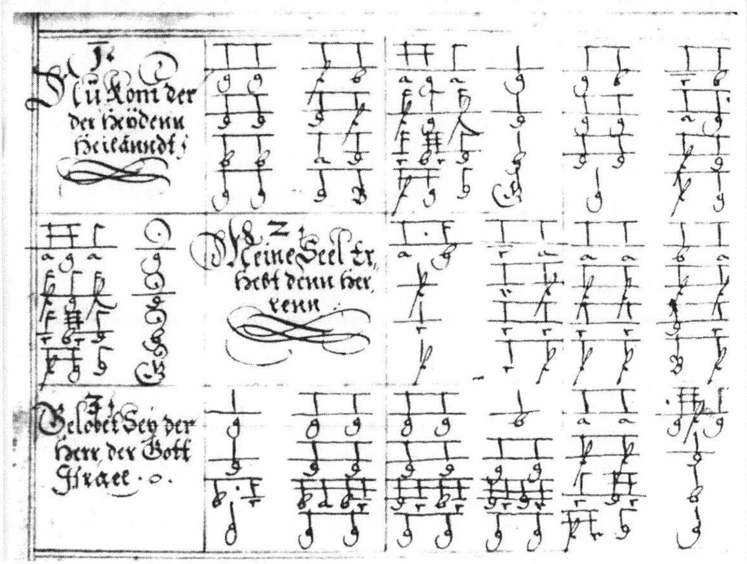

Figure 1. First phrase of "Nun komm, der Heiden Heiland" from August Nörmiger's *Tabulaturbuch auff dem Instrumente* (Dresden,1598). [from microfilm held by Case Western Reserve Library.]

The first tablature that contained multiple settings of Lutheran chorales was *Orgel oder Instrument Tabulatur* (1571) by Elias Nicolaus Ammerbach, organist at the Thomaskirche in Leipzig. While there are many chorales included in this collection, there are only a few that are in current usage in any denomination. Other tablatures are Bernhard Schmid's *Tabulatur Buch...auff Orgeln und Instrumenten zugebrauchen* (Strasbourg, 1577) and Jacob Paix's *Orgel Tabulaturbuch*, 1583, the latter of which gives indications for adding ornamentation.

August Nörmiger's *Tabulaturbuch auff dem Instrumente* (Dresden,1598) is quite remarkable. It contains harmonizations for seventy-seven chorales. The chorale section is organized according to the church year and ends with chorales for the Catechism, the German mass, psalms and other important Lutheran hymns. It begins with the Advent chorale "Nun komm, der Heiden Heiland" and many other familiar chorales, including "Vom Himmel hoch da komm ich her," "O

Mensch, bewein dein Sünde," "Christ lag in Todesbanden," and "Vater unser im Himmelreich" [49] Nearly fifty of these chorales are still in common usage either as congregational chorales in current Lutheran hymnals or as well-known organ chorales. John Butt notes the similarity in the ordering of chorales between Normiger's collection and Bach's *Orgelbüchlein*, which was composed over a century later, calling it "a veritable chorale-book for keyboard."[50]

It should be noted that all of these early tablatures contain chorale settings, but also settings of secular songs and instrumental dances. The chorale settings may have been used as intonations, but the tablatures had a broader use for the keyboardist in the home. Certainly, they were a way to learn many of the chorales that were being sung in church services.

In the 17th century the organ found a new role as an accompaniment instrument to singing, but composers continued to make use of the organ in alternation with choirs. Two of the most prominent composers of the early 17th century, Heinrich Scheidemann (1596–1663) and Samuel Scheidt (1587–1654), composed *alternatim* settings for the liturgy, primarily the *Kyrie* in the Mass, and more importantly the *Magnificat*, which was sung in Vespers. Scheidemann, from the north German city of Hamburg, and Scheidt, from Halle in Saxony, are interesting in that both studied with Jan Pieterszoon Sweelinck in Amsterdam, the noted "maker of German organists." However, each composer reflected the customs and stylistic language of his particular region of origin. In addition to various kinds of settings of chorales (including ornamented chorales and motet-style treatments with the chorale melody in the bass), Scheidemann's organ works include a number of *praeludia*, which feature an opening and closing free and a fugal or otherwise imitative section in the middle. In succeeding generations, this form

49 Merian, Wilhelm. *Der Tanz in den deutschen Tabulaturbüchern*. (Hildesheim: Georg Olms. 1968), 220.

50 Butt, 163-164.

blossomed into the North German *praeludia* of Dieterich Buxtehude and many others.

By contrast, Samuel Scheidt is known for his large body of vocal compositions which range from works for a single voice to pieces for multiple choirs of 8 to 12 voices. His organ contributions are even more significant, in that he followed Sweelinck's lead in developing the chorale variation. His *Tabulatura nova* (1624) in three volumes comprises settings of Lutheran chorales, folk tunes, fantasias, and *Magnificat* settings. It is a "new" tablature in that it is written in conventional five-line staff notation, with each part placed on a separate staff. However, in his edition *Tabulatura nova,* Harald Vogel notes that the "new" refers to the type of repertoire contained within the collection.[51] In any event, the third part of *Tabulatura nova* contains "the most extensive collection of liturgical music intended for the Lutheran church service printed in its time."[52] Scheidt gives descriptions for each of the variations, for example *Choralis in cantu, Choralis in bass colorato* (ornamented). The fact that he labels each "versus" may indicate that the chorale settings were intended for alternation use in congregational singing. The *Magnificat* settings (9 settings, one on each of the tones) most assuredly are intended for congregational use. There are six organ versets on each tone for the twelve verses of the *Magnificat* text.

Scheidt's last contribution to the organ literature was the *Tabulatur-Buch Hundert geistlicher Lieder und Psalmen Herrn Doctoris Martini Lutheri und anderer gottseligen Männer*(1650), often called the *Görlitz Tabulaturbuch* because it was commissioned by the town of Görlitz. As an example of the new and expanded role of the organ in accompanying congregational singing, it contains one hundred straightforward four-part settings, all with the melody in the soprano, all suitable for playing on the organ (or instruments) as the

51 Harald Vogel, ed. Samuel Scheidt. Tabulatura nova, Part II (Wiesbaden: Edition Breitkopf 8566, 1998), 7.

52 Harald Vogel, ed. Samuel Scheidt, Tabulatura nova, part III (Wiesbaden: Edition Breitkopf 8567, 2001), 182.

congregation sang the chorale. This format has been used in hymnals from the 17th century to the present day.

How might the organ have come to "accompany" the singing of the hymns?

The development toward the organ as an accompaniment to the singing of hymns comes from a choral repertoire with the publication of Lucas Osiander's *Fünffzig geistliche Lieder und Psalmen* (Nuremberg, 1586). Osiander's collection may be considered the first collection of true four-part chorales. He used a strictly chordal, note-for-note ("cantional") style rather than a contrapuntal style to provide harmonies for the traditional Lutheran chorale melodies. To further encourage congregational singing—and perhaps more significantly—he moved the chorale melody from its normal location in the tenor voice to the soprano so that it could be more easily heard by the congregation.

Several documents note the use of the organ as accompaniment within the decade following Osiander's publication. Joseph Herl notes that in Danzig, Prussia (now Gdansk, Poland) in 1589-90, the Reformed movement gained control of several churches in the city. Along with many changes to conform to Reformed practice (for example, the elimination of paintings in the church), Latin motets that had been sung were replaced with metrical psalms. The psalms were sung "in four parts in the choir, and the organ was played with them."[53] This would have been a departure from what we understand as the earlier Reformed practice of unison singing, but perhaps was done to please those who liked music. Herl notes that "in the choir" may mean the location within the church building and not necessarily "by the choir."

In an *Order for Singing in the Choir and in the Church* for St. Katherine's also in Danzig (1601), there is a direction for the singing of two communion hymns/psalms: "on the first

53 Joseph Herl, *Worship Wars in Early Lutheranism: Choir, Congregations, and Three Centuries of Conflict* (New York: Oxford University Press, 2004), 132.

Sunday, the first psalm, *Gott sei gelobet und gebenedeit,* and on the following Sunday the second, *Jesus Christus, unser Heiland,* in their entirety shall be sung and simultaneously played on the organ."[54] Apparently, this was concession by or to the council, since these hymns had been sung regularly before reforms had been made.

In 1604, the *Melodeyen Gesangbuch* was published in Hamburg. It included four-part settings of hymn tunes in the cantional style composed by the organists of the four city churches: Hieronymus Praetorius, Joachim Decker, Jacob Praetorius, David Scheidemann. The preface to the hymnal notes specifically that the organ was used to accompany congregational singing in the Hamburg churches.[55] However, it should be noted that these settings were published in choir-book format, that is, soprano and tenor parts separately on the left page; alto and bass also separately on the right page. The organist in Hamburg would need to transcribe the setting for organ, perhaps in tablature. Joseph Herl notes that several organists (there) complained about the duties of having to "accompany" the hymns, which likely refers to the process of having to write out the harmonizations.

In 1617, the city of Rostock celebrated the one hundredth anniversary of the Reformation. For the festive service, the organ participated by accompanying the congregation. The parts of the liturgy with the organ are described as follows:

> *Allein Gott in der Höh sei Her* sung figurally [that is, polyphonically by the choir] after the Latin *Gloria* with organ accompaniment;
>
> *O Herre Gott, dein göttlich Wort* sung figurally after the Epistle with the organ and the entire congregation;
>
> *Nun lobe, meine Seele, den Herrn* and other German psalms sung at unspecified places with the organ and the entire congregation;

54 Leaver and Zager, 19.

55 Ibid., 20.

> The *Magnificat* at Vespers sung figurally with organ, with the entire congregation joining in the German *Te Deum* of Luther; and
>
> *Nun lobe, meine Seele, den Herrn* sung figurally after the Vespers sermon with the organ and the entire congregation.[56]

While the Reformation movement called for modifications in both the mass and the offices, the immediate effect upon the organ was fairly minor. Practices varied from location to location, but the use of the organ to introduce choral or congregational singing or to play in alternation continued for the most part. With the beginning of the cantional style toward the end of the 16th century, the organ began to be seen as a useful tool to accompany the congregation in its song. In the following generations, the organ could be used either in alternation or as an accompaniment instrument for congregational singing, but the expanding role of the organ was decidedly in favor of providing accompaniment for the congregation.

56 Herl, 133.

Bibliography

Becker, Cecil Warren. *A Transcription of Elias Nikolaus Ammerbach's Orgel oder Instrument Tabulaturbuch, Second Edition (1583) Volume II.* D.M.A. dissertation, U of Rochester, Eastman School of Music, 1963.

Bush, Douglas Earl, *The Liturgical Use of the Organ in German Regions Prior to the Protestant Reformation: Contracts, Consuetudinaries, and Musical Repertories*, Ph. D. dissertation, University of Texas at Austin, 1982.

Butt, John, "Germany and the Netherlands," in Alexander Silbiger, ed. *Keyboard Music Before 1700.* New York: Schirmer Books, An Imprint of Simon & Schuster Macmillan, 1995.

Gotsch, Herbert, "The Organ in the Lutheran Service of the 16th Century," *Church Music 67.1*, (St. Louis, Mo: Concordia Publishing House, 1967), pp. 7-12.

Herl, Joseph, *Worship Wars in Early Lutheranism: Choir, Congregations, and Three Centuries of Conflict.* New York: Oxford University Press, 2004.

Leaver, Robin A. and Daniel Zager, *Organ Accompaniment of Congregational Song: Historical Documents and Settings, Parts 1 and 2.* (*Historical Organ Techniques and Repertoire*, volumes 12 and 13), Colfax, NC: Wayne Leupold Editions, 2017.

Marshall, Robert L. and Robin A. Leaver. "Chorale settings." *Grove Music Online. Oxford Music Online.* Oxford University Press, accessed October 25, 2016, http://www.oxfordmusiconline.com/subscriber/article/grove/music/05663

McConnell, Harlan. 1975. "The Sixteenth-Century German Keyboard Chorale." In *Church Music 75.1* (St. Louis, Mo: Concordia Publishing House, 1975), 14-22.

Merian, Wilhelm. *Der Tanz in den deutschen Tabulaturbüchern*. Leipzig 1927; reprint, Hildesheim: Georg Olms. 1968.

Porter, William, "Hamburg Organists in Lutheran Worship," in Kerala J. Snyder, ed., *The Organ as a Mirror of Its Time,* 60-77. New York: Oxford University Press, 2002.

Vogel, Harald, ed. Samuel Scheidt. *Tabulatura nova, in Three Parts*. Wiesbaden: Edition Breitkopf (Nos. 8565, 8566, 8567), 1994, 1998, and 2001.

About the Authors

Daniel Zager is Associate Dean and Head of Sibley Music Library; Associate Professor of Musicology; and Affiliate Faculty Member in the Organ, Sacred Music, and Historical Keyboards Department at the Eastman School of Music, where he teaches courses in the history and practice of sacred music. He earned the Ph.D. degree in musicology from the University of Minnesota. His monograph *The Gospel Preached Through Music: The Purpose and Practice of Lutheran Church Music* was published by Concordia Theological Seminary Press in 2013, and won an "Award of Commendation" from the Concordia Historical Institute in 2014. His most recent publications, in collaboration with Robin A. Leaver, are two volumes entitled *Organ Accompaniment of Congregational Song: Historical Documents and Settings*, vol.1 covering the sixteenth and seventeenth centuries in Germany and England, vol. 2 covering eighteenth-century Germany (Wayne Leupold Editions, 2017).

Steven Wente is distinguished professor of music and organist to the Chapel of Our Lord at Concordia University Chicago, River Forest, Illinois, where he serves as chair of the music department, coordinates graduate programs in music, and teaches organ and courses in music history. He currently also serves as cantor at First Saint Paul's

Lutheran Church, Chicago. His undergraduate and graduate degrees are from Concordia, River Forest. He earned the doctor of music degree in organ performance from Northwestern University. He has performed widely across the country, and has written for several journals, including the *Concordia Historical Institute Quarterly* and *Lutheran Forum*.